BOOK ANALYSIS

Written by Valérie Nigdélian-Fabre
Translated by Rose Brichard

AF143843

Antigone

BY SOPHOCLES

Bright
≡Summaries.com

SOPHOCLES

GREEK PLAYWRIGHT

- **Born in Athens in roughly 496 BC**
- **Died in Athens in roughly 406 BC**
- **Notable works:**
    - *Antigone* (roughly 442 BC), tragedy
    - *Philoctetes* (409 BV), tragedy
    - *Oedipus at Colonus* (401 JC - published posthumously), tragedy

Along with Aeschylus and Euripides, Sophocles is one of the most well-known tragedians of ancient Greece. He was born in roughly 496 BC and died in roughly 406 BC. During his life-time, he wrote more than one hundred tragedies, only seven of which have been preserved until the present day. These tragedies include *Oedipus the King* and *Antigone.* Unlike his predecessor Aeschylus, Sophocles' plays place less empha-sis on the chorus (a group of performers who comment on the dramatic action through singing or speaking in unison), and focusses more on the hero's inner thoughts and psyche. In Aristotle's *Poetics*, Sophocles and his work is often cited as the ultimate model of Greek tragedy.

ANTIGONE

THE BIRTH OF THE LEGEND OF OEDIPUS

- **Genre:** play (tragedy)
- **Reference edition:** Sophocles [no date] *Antigone*. [online]. Trans. Fitz, D. and Fitzgerald, R. [Accessed 12 July 2016]. Available from: <https://mthoyibi.files.wordpress.com/2011/05/antigone_2.pdf>
- **First edition:** roughly 442 BC
- **Themes:** mythology, destiny, revolution, duality, love, power, death.

First performed around 442 BC, *Antigone* is without a doubt the most celebrated of all Greek tragedies. Throughout the ages it has remained relevant, often through reinterpretation and reinvention. *Antigone* is the last of Sophocles' Theban plays, a cycle of three plays featuring *Oedipus the King* and *Oedipus at Colonus*. In *Antigone*, Sophocles' writing shows an expectation that the audience have some prior knowledge of the story developed in the preceding plays.

The play revolves around Antigone, Oedipus' daughter/sister, and the terrible fate which awaits her. With her brothers Eteocles and Polyneices having killed each other in a power struggle to rule Thebes, Creon has ruled that Polyneices will not be buried and lie dead on the battlefield. Antigone defies him and sanctifies Polyneices' body with holy rites. Through various developments, she is eventually condemned to death for her actions, and therefore shows herself as the embodiment of dissidence in the face of the establishment.

SUMMARY

The play opens on the day after Eteocles and Polyneices, Oedipus' two sons, have killed each other in the Thebes civil war. Antigone tells her sister Ismene that their uncle Creon, henceforth the king of Thebes, has ordered that Polyneices' body not be buried or receive any funeral rites. Antigone is determined to defy Creon's orders, ready to risk her life in doing so.

PARODOS: THE ENTRANCE OF THE CHORUS

The chorus tells the story of the mortal combat which Thebes had emerged victorious from. Since their father had been exiled (Sophocles outlines that story in *Oedipus at Colonus*), Eteocles and Polyneices had agreed to share the responsibility for the Theban throne by taking it in turns to rule for one year at a time. This was supposed to be a solution to Oedipus' curse, which predicted they would kill one another. Yet when the time came, Eteocles refused to give up the crown and his brother Polyneices responded by forming an army of seven men to wage war against the city of Thebes (Aeschylus tells a detailed version of this story in his play *Seven Against Thebes*, 467 BC). All but one of the men died in combat, alongside the two "brothers in blood / Face to face in matchless rage / Mirroring each the other's death / Clashed in long combat." (lines 119-125).

SCENE I

Creon, the newly-proclaimed king of Thebes, outlines his vision and principles for his reign, strongly emphasising the devout patriotism he expects from all subjects. Seeing the late Polyneices as the opposite, someone who waged war on his own city, Creon declares that no-one shall touch Polyneices' body and he will not be buried. His brother Eteocles on the other hand is glorified in his death as a patriot and a hero. When a sentry comes to announce that Polyneices' body has been found covered in dust after being given a symbolic burial, Creon orders the sentry to find the culprit or face being condemned to death himself.

SCENE II

Antigone is arrested when she is found covering Polyneices' body after the guards have uncovered it. Caught at the scene of the crime, a furious Antigone admits to her deed without the slightest hesitation. She stands up to Creon and resolutely defends divine justice, denouncing Creon's orders as arbitrary and immoral. She turns down any help from her sister Ismene, who tries to shift the blame towards herself. In doing so, she saves Ismene's life. Through Ismene, the audience learns that Antigone is engaged to Creon's son Haemon.

SCENE III

Haemon appears on stage. He publicly declares allegiance to his father Creon, though still tries to persuade him not to kill Antigone by telling him that the Theban people are against it. Creon ignores Haemon's arguments, and a rift between them begins to show. Their discussions descend into a bitter argument and Haemon fiercely criticises his father for being obstinate, blind to the truth around him and a tyrant. This acts as a stimulus for reflection on the essence of democracy itself.

After Haemon leaves in a rage, Creon somewhat reduces the punishment he had initially planned for the two sisters. He sets Ismene free and orders that Antigone be buried alive in a tomb instead of being stoned to death.

SCENE IV

Resigned to her fate, Antigone is taken to her living tomb and laments the life as a woman which she will never lead, her life being brutally cut short as a young girl fresh out of childhood.

SCENE V

The blind prophet Tiresias enters and warns Creon that Polyneices' body must be buried quickly as it has offended the gods and will bring misfortune on all Thebes. Creon initially accuses Tiresias of lying and being corrupt, but eventually agrees to the burial after much arguing. Amid the threat of a widespread contagion, he finally orders that Antigone be freed and that Polyneices' body receive funeral rites and a proper burial with the words "The laws of the gods are mighty, and a man must serve them / To the last day of his life!" (lines 879-880).

SCENE VI

A messenger arrives to inform the chorus and Eurydice - Creon's wife and Haemon's mother - of the tragic end that the young lovers have met: Antigone has hanged herself, Haemon tried to attack his father then killed himself before his very eyes. On hearing this, Eurydice retreats in silence.

When he returns to the palace, Creon is forced to accept his terrible mistake, but his fate becomes even worse: Eurydice also commits suicide. For Creon, it's all too late; he is cursed for evermore. He laments his own fate: "I have killed my son and my wife. / I look for comfort; my comfort lies here dead. / Whatever my hands have touched has come to nothing." (lines 1035-1038).

EXODUS: THE EXIT OF THE CHORUS

The chorus reveal the true moral of the story: "There is no happiness where there is no wisdom; / No wisdom but in submission to the gods." (lines 139-140).

CHARACTER STUDY

ANTIGONE

Antigone is Oedipus' sister and his daughter. She is the victim of a curse on a long line of the Labdacids.

She is a young woman and is still a virgin. She is both fragile and strong; she stands alone in the face of danger and Creon's tyranny. Through this, she is the image of both the dutiful daughter (she acts as a tender and loving guide to Oedipus in his exile to Colonus) and of the revolutionary, summed up in the words, "Like father, like daughter: both headstrong, deaf to reason!" (line 375). She champions love against political rationality and idealism against realism; she is virtuous, unmovable and moral. Hegel calls her the most noble creature ever to have walked the earth. However, when Antigone kills herself and chooses the world of the dead, it could be argued that she becomes a sort of fanatical fundamentalist in her death, juxtaposing directly with Creon, the image of nationalism and secularism.

CREON

Creon is the brother of Jocasta, and therefore the natural heir to the throne of Thebes after Oedipus' sons have killed one another. He is initially presented as a figure of absolute power, speaking of the responsibilities and difficulties of governance. The lines, "The man who knows how to obey, and that man only, / Knows how to give commands" (lines 530-1), show him to be the incarnation of social order, civil obedience and discipline. However, he quickly emerges as a merciless tyrant, proud and pig-headed. He turns a blind eye to any opposition, even when it comes from his own son. The only thing which finally forces him to change his ways is the threat of punishment from the gods, but it's already too little too late.

GOOD TO KNOW: THE LABDACIDS

After Europa, daughter of Agenor, was abducted by Zeus who took on the form of a powerful bull, her brother Cadmus set off to look for her. However, following advice given to him by an oracle, Cadmus gave up on his quest to find Europa and instead founded the city of Thebes. He married Harmonia, daughter of Ares and Aphrodite. They had three children: Agave, whose descendants would be Creon and Jocasta, Semele, Dionysus' mother, and Polydros, father of Labdacus. Labdacus' descendants are known as Labdacids; Oedipus was part of this ancestral line. After Labdacus died, his son Laius was taken into the care of the regent Pelops. Laius fell in love with Pelops' son and abducted him - this enraged Hera and she cursed him and all his descendants. Later on, the oracle at Delphi warned him that he must never have children if he wanted to save the city of Thebes and save himself from death. However, Laius did not take this advice and had a son with Jocasta. The child - Oedipus - was abandoned on Mount Cithaeron, but was taken in by a shepherd and adopted by the king and queen of Corinth. As a man, Oedipus heard a dreadful prediction from the oracle at

Delphi that he was going to kill his father and marry his mother. To escape the curse, he fled Corinth and headed for Thebes, unknowingly marching towards his own terrible fate. On the way there he met Laius and killed him in a violent altercation.

When he arrived in Thebes, Oedipus gave a correct answer to the Sphinx's riddle and therefore won the throne and Queen Jocasta's hand in marriage; the prophecy had come true. Thebes was therefore cursed by incest and murder and was plagued by a mysterious epidemic. In the hope of ending the epidemic, Thebes searched for the person who had killed Laius and little by little learned the awful truth. Jocasta hanged herself, unable to bear what had happened. Finding his mother/wife dead, Oedipus blinded himself with her brooch and left Thebes, leaving his sons to fall victim to the curse.

ISMENE

Ismene is Antigone's sister. She is calmer and more contemplative than her sister, ready to obey orders and aware of the consequences of her potential actions. While she is initially pragmatic, she soon risks her own life in the hope of saving her sister.

In previous versions of this story from mythology, Ismene does not feature as a character. However, since Sophocles deals with the conflict arising from Polyneices' body and Creon's orders against it being buried, the invention of

Ismene allows the playwright to raise moral questions about the correct route to follow in such a situation, as well as creating a powerful contrast to Antigone's cruel radicalism.

HAEMON

Haemon had always been a dutiful and respectful son towards his parents Creon and Eurydice until he changes all that by defying his father and defending Antigone, to whom he is engaged. Before killing himself, he spits in his father's face. Haemon is representative of youth, the people and democracy. This is in direct contrast to Creon, the embodiment of age and tyranny. Ismene and Haemon together can be understood as the moderate reflections of Antigone and Creon, the embodiments of radicalism and the true heroes of the action.

THE CHORUS

The chorus is made up of Athenian citizens who are disguised and masked. Their role is to comment on the plot through song and speech, and their interjections punctuate the various scenes of the play. The chorus' words place them at a certain distance from the action and somewhat takes on a life of its own. Through this, the chorus at once becomes the perfect spectator and connects with the universal, as a collective manifestation of the human condition. This universality is particularly resonant in the song about love which follows the dialogue between Haemon and Creon and the ode on the triumph of man over nature.

ANALYSIS

MYTHOLOGY

As is the case with the majority of Greek tragedies which have survived to the present day, Sophocles' *Antigone* is inspired by the founding myths of Greek civilisation, passed down since time immemorial through the oral tradition. The episode of Greek mythology which is most significant with regards to drama is the Trojan War; almost half of the tragedies which have survived the test of time explore this part of history. Sophocles' trilogy, however, tells the story of the Labdacids - the line which began with Cadmus the founder of Thebes - and their cursed destiny. *Antigone* is the third play chronologically, following on from *Oedipus the King*, in which Oedipus discovers the terrible truth, and *Oedipus at Colonus*, in which Oedipus is exiled and dies. Despite this, *Antigone* was in fact written before the other plays, and focusses on one aspect of the myth which had been little explored before Sophocles made it the subject of his work, namely Polyneices' body being condemned to lie unburied and unsanctified.

THE HERO: ALONE AGAINST THE WORLD

Among Sophocles' seven surviving plays, six have epony-mous heroes or heroines, meaning the work is named after one of its characters (*Ajax, Electra, Philoctetes,* etc). Such a dedication shows Sophocles' emphasis on the figure of the individual standing in the face of adversity, unmoving and determined. Sophocles' heroes tend to be solitary and resolute; often they are young women who defy the compromises inherent to coming of age. These radical heroes are set against a backdrop of theatrical innovation which Aristotle attributes to Sophocles: Sophocles added a third actor to his plots where traditionally there were only two. This adds a new dimension of complexity to the storyline and allows for a true exploration of the psychological nuances of the characters. Isolated and obstinate, the Sophoclean hero is destined for tragedy, whether through their own actions or through an attempt to escape the will of the gods. Ajax kills herself despite her family's desperate efforts, Electra takes her desire for vengeance to the deadly extreme and Antigone chooses death over obedience. This destructive radicalism is a combination of free will and fate. It inspires and shapes the powerful mechanisms of tragedy and endows Sophoclean plays with a true sense of the sublime; above the characters in the play are great powers who have absolute authority and may demand the ultimate sacrifice.

ANTIGONE: THE PLAY BUILT ON BINARY OPPOSITION AND DUALITY

Antigone is built around a series of contradictory and irreducible oppositions which flow magnificently through the four agon scenes - the successive scenes in which two characters oppose one another and that explore contrasting values and ideas. Sophocles invented stichomythia - a theatrical device in which two characters speak alternate lines of verse. This allows the playwright to build dramatic tension and for dramatic portrayal of fierce oppositions which seem evermore irreconcilable. For example, when Creon declares, "An enemy is an enemy, even dead." (line 417), Antigone responds with "It is may nature to join in love, not hate." (418). This exchange hurtles towards Creon's dramatic retort: "Go join them, then; if you must have your love, / Find it in hell!" (419-20). The debate inevitably leads to an impossible dialogue which will end in death.

- Ismene and Antigone's argument about burying their dead brother is the first agon scene. While their discussion begins in a tender and loving fashion, it soon descends into violent opposition between Antigone, intent on performing the holy rites on her brother's body despite Creon's orders, and Ismene in her pragmatic fatalism.
- The next confrontation occurs between and Antigone and Creon, and can be read in several lights, giving it even greater importance with regards to Sophocles' masterful drama and poetry. The scene presents the clash between the sacred love between siblings and the rational objectivity of the State - in other words, the law of the gods against earthly social justice and reason. However, it can also be viewed as exploring the opposition between youth and age, in turn linked to political idealism and political realism respectively. Furthermore, there are other thematic dimensions in the scene such as the individual versus society, nature versus culture and even the living versus the dead. Lastly, the scene strongly explores the contours of the opposition between men and women, with Antigone representing liberty from and rage against patriarchal rule. She is, after all, a young girl standing in the face of absolute patriarchal power, asserting her

independence, her free will, and her right to judge events by her own moral compass.

- This is followed by the heated discussion between Haemon and Creon. At first, this is characterised by obedience and solidarity, but soon turns towards rebellion. This illustrates not only a son against his father, but more universally the slave against the tyrant. Haemon quickly leaves behind the role of a dutiful son and rejects his father's arbitrary rule ("It is no City if it takes orders from one voice.", line 597). He goes so far as to viciously insult and threaten his father - "If you were not my father, / I'd say you were perverse." (lines 615-616).

- The final opposition dialogue occurs between Creon and Tiresias, shining the spotlight on men versus gods, and natural order versus divine order. Creon is blinded by hate and is unable to recognise his own guilt, now that Thebes is "stained with the corruption of dogs and carrion birds / That glut themselves on the corpse of Oedipus' son." (lines 798-799). He insults Tiresias and brings another curse upon himself and his family in doing so.

As such, the play illustrates how only disaster can emerge from a system constructed from irreconcilable differences with no possibility to compromise with regards to principles and the use of force.

THE REALMS OF THE LIVING AND THE DEAD

The main controversy in the plot is that of the right to a holy burial and sacred ritual. In the context of the play, these rites are vital for the dead, whose spirits will otherwise be condemned to wander forever more, never at peace. However, they are also of true importance to the living, since an unsanctified corpse brings with it curses from the gods. The threat of maleficent divine intervention looms over the entirety of the play; while Polyneices' body is left to rot in the open, prey for wild bird and dogs, Antigone is buried alive in a tomb. This represents a confusion between the world of the living and the realm of the dead which in turn leaves Thebes as a city infringing upon divine law, thus embodying a true threat to the entire cosmic order. To restore things to normality, Creon must step down.

TRAGIC IRONY

Sophocles is the master of tragic irony. Tragic irony in theatre emerges from the contrast between the audience knowing that a character's actions will lead to tragedy while the character themselves is unaware. This rift between the knowledge of the audience and the protagonist introduces a subtle dialectic between the question of a hero's own agency and divine predestination; while the hero believes themselves to be free, the character is generally shown to be a pawn in the games of the gods. *Oedipus the King* displays a particularly masterful use of tragic irony when Oedipus tries to escape his destiny by fleeing Corinth and his adopted parents (he believes they are instead his biological parents), when in fact he is walking straight towards his own demise and the fulfilment of the prophecy. This irony makes Oedipus' gradual understanding of the situation all the more tragic, towards the moment of horrendous understanding when he blinds himself. Antigone's fate seems also to be written in the stars - she is a descendent of Labdacus and therefore followed by the curse of the Labdacids, thus calling into question her own freedom and her responsibility for her actions, as the cursed child of Oedipus.

FURTHER REFLECTION

SOME QUESTIONS TO THINK ABOUT...

- Jacques Lacan (French psychoanalyst, 1901-1981) calls Antigone the ideal victim in her own choice to be condemned. He has noted that Sophocles sets himself apart from other writers through creating heroes which always finish in last place. Discuss this idea.
- Is Antigone's sacrifice representative of the price which must be paid for rebelling against order?
- How does Sophocles' emphasis on individualism conflict with social ties among his characters? How does this link to the idea of citizenship and how would you define it?
- Antigone breaks with traditional female roles and asserts herself against patriarchal authority. Discuss Ismene's statement. "We are only women, / We cannot fight with men, Antigone!" (line 47-48).
- Antigone is a figure who is in many ways defined by her role in relation to powerful men; the daughter of Oedipus and the fiancée of Haemon. Given these constraints, how does she construct and express her independence?
- Antigone represents a figure of freedom, anarchy, revolution and resistance. Discuss how Sophocles' writing and the structure of the play allow her to embody these concepts.
- How can ancient mythology be relevant in the modern era?
- While Greek tragedy had its cultural peak in Athens, what technical innovations did Sophocles bring to the genre?
- Antigone argues that her "crime is holy" (line 56). Discuss

the concepts of crime and divinity in the play.

- Creon argues that a city must be ruled by an absolute leader, but the play can be viewed as championing another version of Greek democracy - discuss this contrast and the concepts of governance featured in *Antigone*.

We want to hear from you!
Leave a comment on your online library
and share your favourite books on social media!

FURTHER READING

REFERENCE EDITION

- Sophocles [no date] *Antigone*. [online]. Trans. Fitz, D. and Fitzgerald, R. [Accessed 12th July 2016]. Available from: <https://mthoyibi.files.wordpress.com/2011/05/antigone_2.pdf>

ADAPTATIONS

Antigone has been the subject of various reinterpretations and theatrical adaptations, which is testament to its universality and its relevance even today. Some notable examples are:

- Garnier, R. (1580) *Antigone ou la Piété.*
- Rotrou, J. (1637) *Antigone.*
- Alfieri, V. (1776) Antigone. A play focussing on the political dimension of Sophocles' *Antigone.*
- Cocteau, J. (1922) *Antigone*. First modern adaptation of the play.
- Anouilh, J. (1944) *Antigone.*
- Brecht, B. (1948) *Antigone.*
- Bauchau, H. (1997) *Antigone.*

MORE FROM BRIGHTSUMMARIES.COM

- Reading guide - *Oedipus the King* by Sophocles

Bright ≡Summaries.com

More guides to rediscover your love of literature

Animal Farm
BY GEORGE ORWELL

The Stranger
BY ALBERT CAMUS

Harry Potter and the Sorcerer's Stone
BY J.K. ROWLING

The Silence of the Sea
BY VERCORS

Antigone
BY JEAN ANOUILH

The Flowers of Evil
BY BAUDELAIRE

www.brightsummaries.com

Ebook EAN: 9782806280312

Paperback EAN: 9782806282873

Legal Deposit: D/2016/12603/286

Cover: © Primento

Digital conception by Primento, the digital partner of publishers.